JEWEL STERN/PROJECT SKYLINE

Donated to

**Visual Art Degree
Sherkin Island**

MODERN/MODERNE/MODERNISTIC MIAMI BEACH HOTEL ARCHITECTURE/CIRCA 1940

1

Museum of Modern Art, Oxford 1982
First published by the Akron Art Institute 1979

The exhibition consists of 18 black and white 16" x 20" photographs. These are accompanied by mylar sheets of corresponding ink tracings from the original blueprints and also include information on each hotel. Facts and figures were retrieved from the records of the City of Miami Beach Building Department.

Grant aided by the Dade County Council of Arts and Sciences, sponsored by the Bass Museum of Art, City of Miami Beach, with especial thanks to Diane Camber, Acting Director. The Daniel Wolf Press, New York City, have also kindly contributed. The Museum of Modern Art, Oxford, is subsidised by the Arts Council of Great Britain.

TABLE OF CONTENTS

INTRODUCTION

South Miami Beach, Florida, has been described by Paul Goldberger (**New York Times**, 3 Feb. 1979) as "one of the richest collections of 1930's architecture in the world." Built mostly between 1933-41, and located in a condensed area of some 75 small city blocks within easy walking distance of each other, these numerous examples of Streamlined Moderne architecture (mostly small hotels) combine to form a living museum of the style.

Each building was originally designed to advantageously combine an extremely modest construction cost with a heightened flashy, popular and modern appearance to specifically attract a new, solidly middle class group of tourists to this beach area, formerly a resort of the well-to-do.

Inadequate zoning laws that permitted minimum setback from the street, and little space between buildings, provoked a need to assert the individual identity of each hotel. This was resolved not only in the uniqueness of facade detailing, but in many instances by the attachment of ingeniously designed and varied towers rising above the low skyline. They embody jazzy signs, multi-colored neon lighting, fins, and flagpoles set within richly ornamental finials.

The towers, like the facades below are built of cast, banded, carved, and/or painted concrete and stucco, often with fluted elements to accentuate strong directional movements. A wide variety of modern materials were used, such as chrome, stainless steel, glass block, cast stone, vitrolite and plastic. Despite a certain coarseness of detailing, it is the versatility and inventiveness of the architects, their freedom to use any kind of fantasy, that gives each building its own expressive edge.

Jewel Stern has known these buildings since her childhood. It was her intention to document them. But her 18 photographs so elegantly and succinctly capture the spirit of the architecture that they stand as a work of art in themselves.

John Coplans

ARTIST'S STATEMENT

My father was in the hotel business before I was born. In 1935 he and my mother decided to move to Miami Beach for the winter tourist season. Every subsequent winter of their lives and mine were spent in Florida. Summers were generally spent in upstate New York where the family had a summer resort. Dad operated hotels on Miami Beach until he died in 1977. Ironically, although he operated more than a dozen hotels on the Beach over the years, not one of them fit the criteria I had set for **Project Skyline**.

As a child of elementary and junior high school age, I remember that we often took a "ride" in the car along the ocean front just to see what was going on. It was a kind of excursion, seeing all the new development. Up until I was about 14 we lived on South Beach. Also, I remember being fiercely defensive about Miami Beach as a hometown – as atypical as it was!

From the time I was 22 I have lived in Coral Gables. The (Miami) Beach became much less significant in my life as the years passed. And, of course, it changed. During the spring of 1976 I began to look at the architecture on Miami Beach and to see it in a different light. This was probably a result, as least partially, of the increased interest in Art Deco and the number of publications and articles which appeared on the style in the early seventies. Also, I had begun my research on Ely Jacques Kahn, a New York City architect who excelled in commercial buildings in the Art Deco style in the late 1920s. I began exploring South Beach on foot during the summer of 1976 and making notes. The Project evolved from this beginning.

I want to acknowledge the assistance of Barbara M. Schwartz and Denis Arden in photography and architecture, respectively. Finally, I want to recognize my father, Jack Muravchick, who in a way has been my "silent partner" in this enterprise. He had the kind of buoyant optimism and faith in the future that was so characteristic of the men and women who ventured south to seek their fortunes on Miami Beach.

Jewel Stern
9/15/79

Note: Seventeen of the hotels selected for inclusion in the project were built during the boom of the late 1930s and prior to World War II (December 1941). The authenticity these hotels still retain qualified them in a general sense. Specifically, each building displayed a prominent tower or a facade which incorporated a tower-like projection. Isolated, these upper reaches remained virtually unaffected by the modification campaigns of successive owners. A chronological departure was made in the case of the eighteenth hotel, a post-war example, which exhibits strong references to the selected group.

ALBERT ANIS

Born:	April 18, 1889 in Chicago, Illinois
Died:	August 28, 1964 in Miami Beach, Florida
Education:	Armour Institute of Technology, Chicago 1908-1910
Certificate: Date Certified:	#690 January 16, 1926 (cancelled November 30, 1929)
Certificate: Date Certified:	#1004 January 12, 1935

Pre-World War II Hotels: Abbey*
Berkeley Shore*
Avalon
Bancroft
Clevelander
James
Leslie
Majestic
Olympic
Poinciana
Tyler
Waldorf Towers
Whitelaw
Winterhaven

*photographed

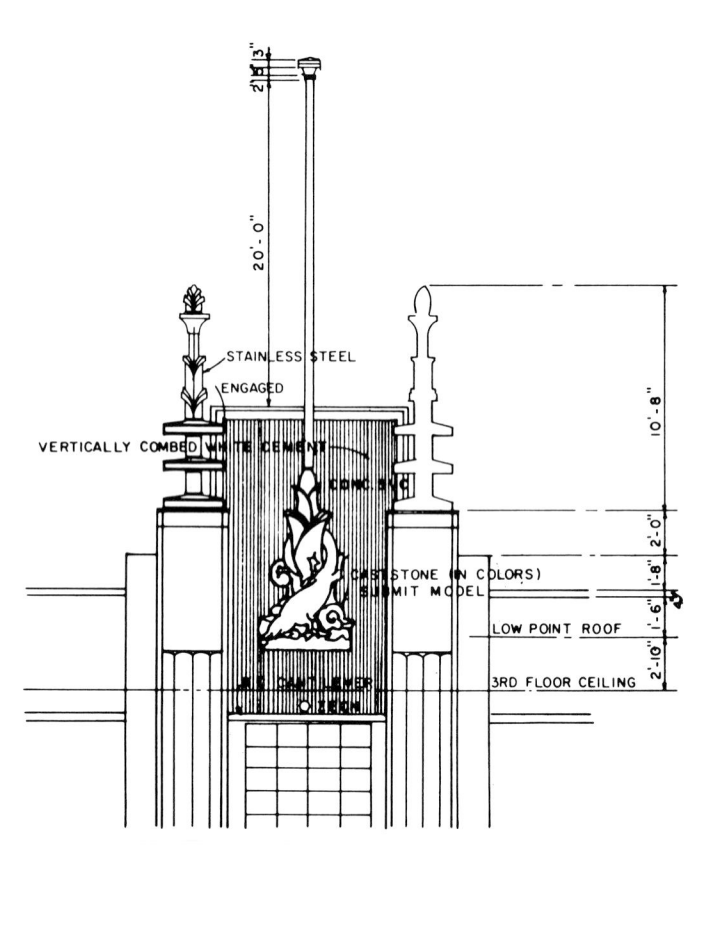

ABBEY HOTEL
300 21st Street

Permit: #14833

Date: October 15, 1940

Subdivision: Miami Beach Improvement Company Ocean Front

Architect: Albert Anis

General Contractor: Pollack Construction Company

Owner: Knox Corporation

Rooms: 2 rooms and 24 apartments

Cost: $80,000

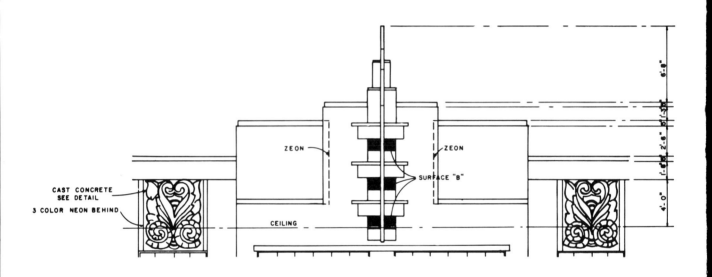

CAST CONCRETE
SEE DETAIL

3 COLOR NEON BEHIND

ZEON

ZEON

SURFACE "B"

CEILING

6'-8"

2'-6"

4'-0"

BERKELEY SHORE HOTEL
1610 Collins Avenue

Permit:	#14411
Date:	August 5, 1940
Subdivision:	Fisher's First
Architect:	Albert Anis
General Contractor:	Lux Construction Company
Owner:	Polly Lux
Rooms:	66
Cost:	$90,000

L. MURRAY DIXON

Born: February 16, 1901 in Live Oak, Florida

Died: October 8, 1949 in New York City

Education: Georgia Institute of Technology, Atlanta 1918-1919

Certificate: #946

Date Certified: January 16, 1931

Pre-World War II Hotels: Adams*
                          Beach Plaza*
                          Ritz Plaza*
                          Tiffany*
                          Victor*
                          Fairmont
                          Haddon Hall
                          Kent
                          Marlin
                          McAlpin
                          Palmer House
                          Premier
                          Raleigh
                          Senator
                          Tides
                          Tudor

*photographed

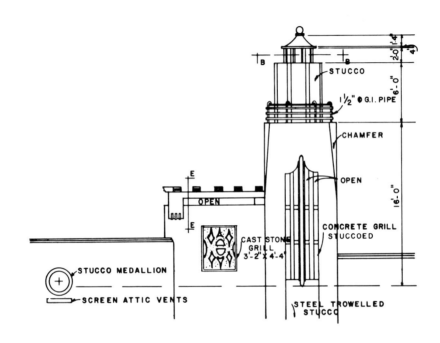

STUCCO

1½" ⌀ G.I. PIPE

CHAMFER

OPEN

OPEN

CONCRETE GRILL
STUCCOED

CAST STONE
GRILL
3'-2" X 4'-4"

STEEL TROWELLED
STUCCO

STUCCO MEDALLION

SCREEN ATTIC VENTS

ADAMS HOTEL
2030 Park Avenue

Permit:	#11238
Date:	June 7, 1938
Subdivision:	Miami Beach Improvement Company Ocean Front
Architect:	L. Murray Dixon
General Contractor:	Fred Howland, Inc.
Owner:	Cameo Corporation
Rooms:	10 rooms and 25 apartments
Cost:	$76,000

TOWER DETAIL DOES NOT APPEAR ON BLUEPRINTS

BEACH PLAZA HOTEL
1401 Collins Avenue

Permit:	#8217
Date:	May 5, 1936
Subdivision:	Ocean Beach #2
Architect:	L. Murray Dixon
General Contractor:	O'Neill and Orr Building Corporation
Owner:	Beach Plaza Corporation
Rooms:	55
Cost:	$66,000

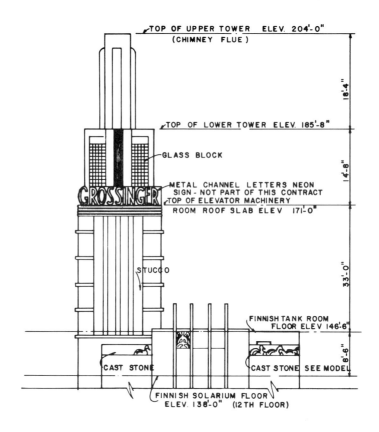

TOP OF UPPER TOWER ELEV. 204'-0"
(CHIMNEY FLUE)

18'-4"

TOP OF LOWER TOWER ELEV. 185'-8"

GLASS BLOCK

14'-8"

METAL CHANNEL LETTERS NEON
SIGN - NOT PART OF THIS CONTRACT
TOP OF ELEVATOR MACHINERY
ROOM ROOF SLAB ELEV. 171'-0"

GROSSINGER

STUCCO

33'-0"

FINNISH TANK ROOM
FLOOR ELEV. 146'-6"

CAST STONE

8'-6"

CAST STONE SEE MODEL

FINNISH SOLARIUM FLOOR
ELEV. 138'-0" (12TH FLOOR)

RITZ PLAZA HOTEL
1701 Collins Avenue

Permit:	#14398
Date:	August 1, 1940
Subdivision:	Fisher's First
Architect:	L. Murray Dixon
General Contractor:	L & H Miller Construction Company
Owner:	Joseph Edell
Rooms:	127 rooms and 2 penthouse apartments
Cost:	$303,000

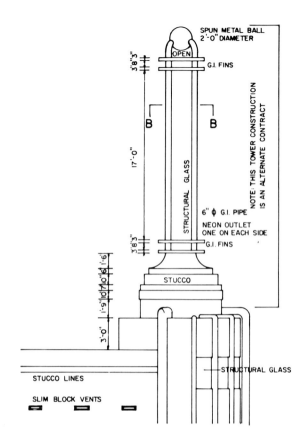

SPUN METAL BALL
2'-0" DIAMETER

OPEN

G.I. FINS

B   B

17'-0"

STRUCTURAL GLASS

NOTE: THIS TOWER CONSTRUCTION IS AN ALTERNATE CONTRACT

6" φ G.I. PIPE

NEON OUTLET
ONE ON EACH SIDE

G.I. FINS

STUCCO

STRUCTURAL GLASS

STUCCO LINES

SLIM BLOCK VENTS

3'-8'3"

3'-8'3"

1'-9" 10"7"10" 9" 1'-6"

3'-0"

TIFFANY HOTEL

801 Collins Avenue

Permit:	#12429
Date:	April 29, 1939
Subdivision:	Ocean Beach #1
Architect:	L. Murray Dixon
General Contractor:	P. J. Davis Construction Company
Owner:	Morris Katz
Rooms:	65
Cost:	$92,000

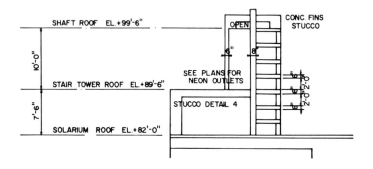

SHAFT ROOF EL.+99'-6"

OPEN

CONC. FINS
STUCCO

10'-0"

SEE PLANS FOR
NEON OUTLETS

STAIR TOWER ROOF EL.+89'-6"

6"

8"

7'-6"

STUCCO DETAIL 4

2'-0" 2'-0"

SOLARIUM ROOF EL.+82'-0"

VICTOR HOTEL
1144 Ocean Drive

Permit:	#10208
Date:	August 24, 1937
Subdivision:	Ocean Beach #2
Architect:	L. Murray Dixon
General Contractor:	L & H Miller Construction Company
Owner:	Astor Holding Company, Louis Miller, President
Rooms:	103
Cost:	$175,000

ROY F. FRANCE

Born:	October 6, 1888 in Hawley, Minnesota
Died:	February 15, 1972 in Miami Beach, Florida
Education:	Armour Institute of Technology, Chicago, Illinois 1905-1906 Chicago Technical School, 2 years of night school? (records unobtainable)
Certificate:	#943
Date Certified:	January 16, 1931

Pre-World War II Hotels:
Cadillac*
National*
Sands*
St. Moritz*
Versailles*
Cavalier
Jefferson
Ocean Grande
Patrician (All Seasons)
Sea Isle
Shoremede (demolished)
White House
Whitman (demolished)

*photographed

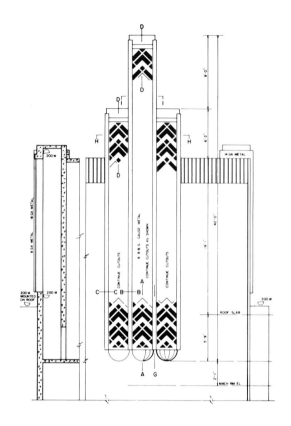

CADILLAC HOTEL
3925 Collins Avenue

Permit:	#14243
Date:	June 25, 1940
Subdivision:	Miami Beach Improvement Company Ocean Front
Architect:	Roy F. France
General Contractor:	P. J. Davis Construction Company
Owner:	Cadillac Corporation
Rooms:	106 rooms and 1 apartment
Cost:	$280,000

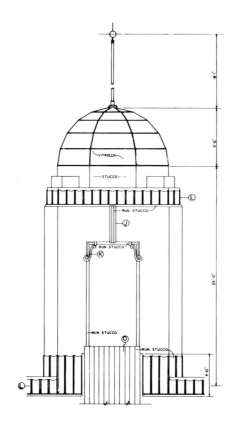

NATIONAL HOTEL
1677 Collins Avenue

Permit:	#14298
Date:	July 11, 1940
Subdivision:	Fisher's First
Architect:	Roy F. France
General Contractor:	Samuel E. Haber
Owner:	Harry Koretsky
Rooms:	106 rooms and 1 apartment
Cost:	$220,000

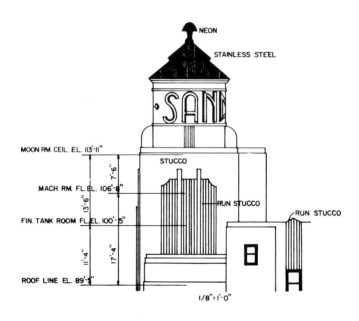

SANDS HOTEL
1601 Collins Avenue

Permit:	#12748
Date:	July 27, 1939
Subdivision:	Fisher's First
Architect:	Roy F. France
General Contractor:	J. Albert and Son
Owner:	Sands Hotel Corporation
Rooms:	100
Cost:	$170,000

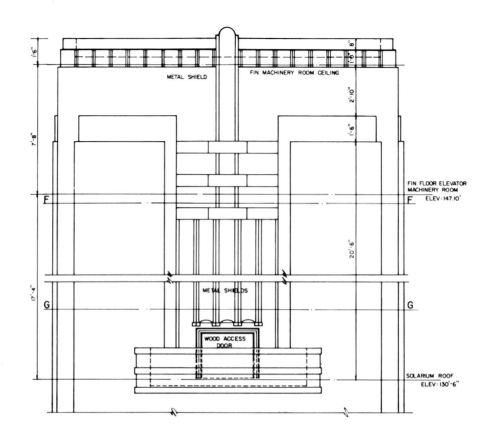

METAL SHIELD   FIN. MACHINERY ROOM CEILING

FIN. FLOOR ELEVATOR
MACHINERY ROOM
F   ELEV: 147.10'

METAL SHIELDS

WOOD ACCESS
DOOR

SOLARIUM ROOF
ELEV: 130'-6"

ST. MORITZ HOTEL
1565 Collins Avenue

Permit:	#12520
Date:	May 25, 1939
Subdivision:	Fisher's First
Architect:	Roy F. France
General Contractor:	W. B. Smith
Owner:	St. Moritz Hotel Co.
Rooms:	130 rooms, 21 penthouses and 2 efficiencies
Cost:	$250,000

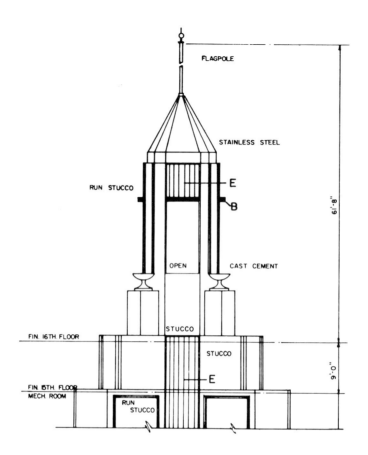

FLAGPOLE

STAINLESS STEEL

RUN STUCCO

E

B

OPEN CAST CEMENT

FIN. 16TH. FLOOR

STUCCO

STUCCO

FIN. 15TH. FLOOR
MECH. ROOM

E

RUN STUCCO

6'-8"

9'-0"

VERSAILLES HOTEL
3425 Collins Avenue

Permit:	#14269
Date:	July 1, 1940
Subdivision:	Miami Beach Improvement Company Ocean Front
Architect:	Roy F. France
General Contractor:	Peter Nordyke
Owner:	Versailles Hotel
Rooms:	141 rooms and 1 apartment
Cost:	$300,000

HENRY HOHAUSER

Born: May 27, 1895 in New York City

Died: March 31, 1963 in Lawrence, Long Island, New York

Education: Pratt Institute graduate, Brooklyn, New York?
                               (Registrar unable to confirm)

Certificate: #1007

Date Certified: January 12, 1935

Pre-World War II Hotels: Collins Park*   Essex House
                               Governor*   Greenview
                               Greystone*   Liberty Arms (Fillard East)
                               Adelphia (Davis)   Mayfair
                               Allen   Neron
                               Cardoza   New Yorker
                               Carlton   Park Central
                               Century   Shepley
                               Colony   Surf
                               Commodore   Surrey
                               Crescent   Webster

*photographed

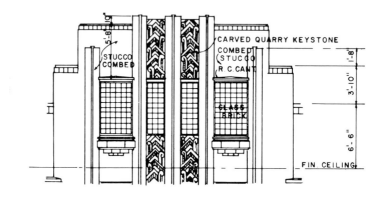

COLLINS PARK HOTEL
2000 Park Avenue

Permit:	#12462
Date:	May 8, 1939
Subdivision:	Miami Beach Improvement Company Ocean Front
Architect:	Henry Hohauser
General Contractor:	J. Y. Gooch Co. Inc.
Owner:	The 2000 Park Avenue Corporation
Rooms:	58
Cost:	$77,000

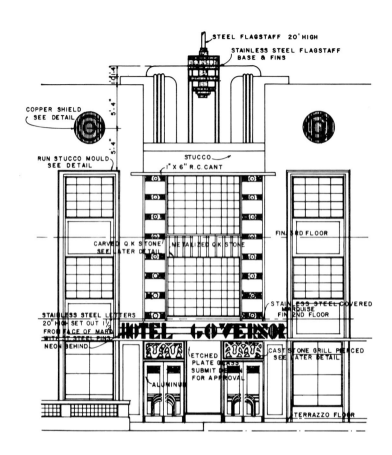

GOVERNOR HOTEL

435 21st Street

Permit:	#12621
Date:	June 21, 1939
Subdivision:	Ocean Park
Architect:	Henry Hohauser
General Contractor:	Stone Builders, Inc.
Owner:	Sam Brody
Rooms:	130
Cost:	$130,000

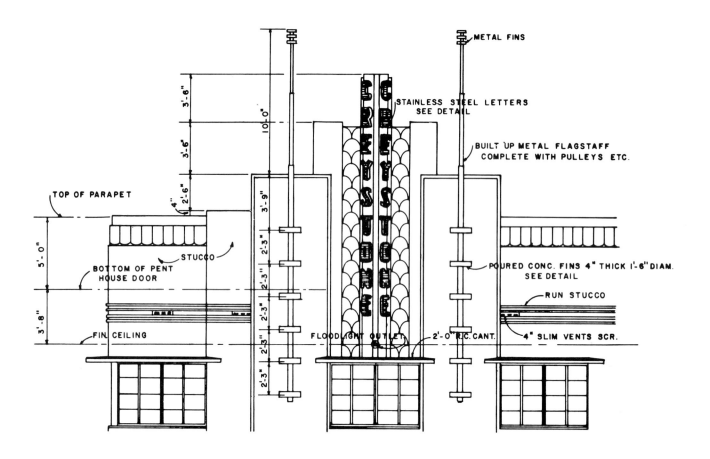

GREYSTONE HOTEL
1920 Collins Avenue

Permit:	#13020
Date:	October 2, 1939
Subdivision:	Miami Beach Improvement Company Ocean Front
Architect:	Henry Hohauser
General Contractor:	Masterbilt Corporation
Owner:	Greystone Hotel
Rooms:	61
Cost:	$80,000

ANTON SKISLEWICZ

Born:	September 28, 1895 in Dubruvnik, Yugoslavia
	Presently living in Longview, Texas (1979)
Education:	Columbia University, New York City
	Bachelor of Architecture, June 5, 1929
Certificate:	#987
Date Certified:	June 16, 1934
Pre-World War II Hotels:	Breakwater*
	Plymouth*
	Corsair
	Kenmore

*photographed

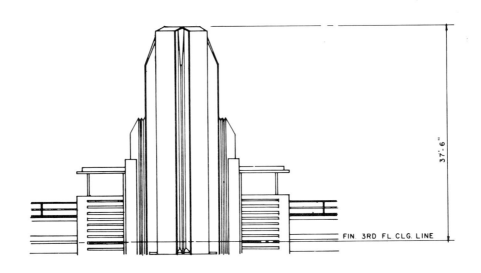

FIN. 3RD FL. CLG. LINE

37'-6"

BREAKWATER HOTEL
940 Ocean Drive

Permit:	#12650
Date:	July 1, 1939
Subdivision:	Ocean Beach #2
Architect:	Anton Skislewicz
General Contractor:	Morris Alpert
Owner:	Aranal Incorporated
Rooms:	75
Cost:	$110,000

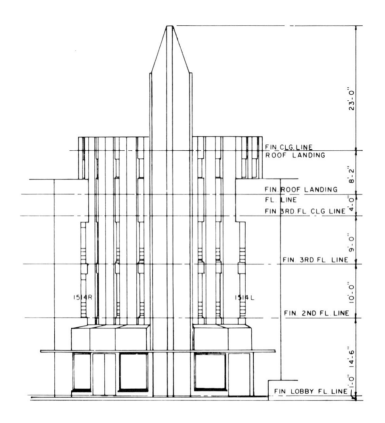

FIN CLG LINE
ROOF LANDING

23'-0"

FIN ROOF LANDING
FL LINE
FIN 3RD FL CLG LINE

8'-2"

4'-0"

FIN 3RD FL LINE

9'-0"

1514R   1514L

FIN 2ND FL LINE

10'-0"

FIN LOBBY FL LINE

14'-6"

1'-0"

PLYMOUTH HOTEL
336 21st Street

Permit:	#14157
Date:	June 6, 1940
Subdivision:	Miami Beach Improvement Company Ocean Front
Architect:	Anton Skislewicz
General Contractor:	Morris Alpert
Owner:	Atlantic Park Corporation
Rooms:	80
Cost:	$100,000

B. ROBERT SWARTBURG

Born: July 27, 1895 in Bucharest, Roumania

Died: December 7, 1975 in Miami Beach, Florida

Education: Columbia University, New York City, 1917-1918
                            Beaux Arts Institute of Design, New York City? (records unobtainable)
                            American Academy in Rome? (reported, but unconfirmed)
                            Ecole des Beaux Arts, Fontainebleau, France? (records unobtainable)

Certificate: #433

Date Certified: June 13, 1925

Post-World War II Hotel: Delano*

*photographed

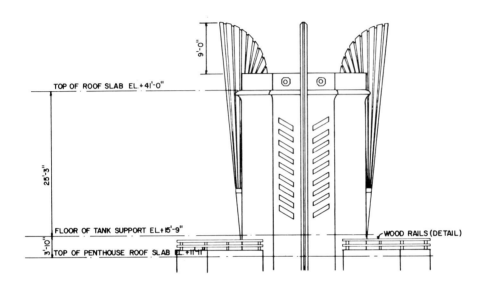

TOP OF ROOF SLAB EL.+41'-0"

9'-0"

25'-3"

FLOOR OF TANK SUPPORT EL.+15'-9"

WOOD RAILS (DETAIL)

3'-10"

TOP OF PENTHOUSE ROOF SLAB EL.+11'-11"

DELANO HOTEL   (postscript)
1685 Collins Avenue

Permit:	#26078
Date:	November 10, 1947
Subdivision:	Fisher's First
Architect:	B. Robert Swartburg
General Contractor:	J. Y. Gooch Inc.
Owner:	Benhow Realty Corporation (Morris Schwartz)
Rooms:	201 rooms and 3 one-bedroom apartments
Cost:	$1,300,000

ARTIST'S BIOGRAPHY

Jewel Stern was born in Brooklyn, New York, in 1934, and has been a resident of Florida since 1935. She attended the University of Miami at Coral Gables (B.A., 1954), and her master's thesis (1978) was on architect Ely Jacques Kahn (The Modernist Years 1925-1931 New York City). Between 1973 and 1979 she has continuously exhibited in one- person and group exhibitions.

BIBLIOGRAPHY

OLD MIAMI BEACH

Ballinger, Kenneth. **Miami Millions.** Miami, Florida: The Franklin Press, 1936.

"Boom Over Miami Beach". **The Architectural Forum** 73 (December 1940): 10.

Fisher, Jane. **Fabulous Hoosier.** New York: Robert M. McBride & Company, 1947.

Lummus, J.N. **The Miracle of Miami Beach.** Miami, Florida: Miami Post Publishing Company, 1940.

Mehling, Harold. **The Most of Everything; The Story of Miami Beach.** New York: Harcourt, Brace and Company, 1960.

Nash, Charles Edgar. **The Magic of Miami Beach.** Philadelphia: David McKay Company, 1938.

"Pleasure Dome". **Time** 35 (February 19, 1940): 18-21.

Redford, Polly. **Billion-Dollar Sandbar; A Biography of Miami Beach.** New York: E.P. Dutton & Company, 1970.

MIAMI BEACH: RECENT NEWSPAPERS and PERIODICALS

Capitman, Barbara Baer. "Re-discovery of Art Deco". **American Preservation** 1 (August/September 1978): 30-41.

Edwards, Ellen. "Art Deco's Curved Walls, Pastels Give Form to Planners' Fantasies". **The Miami Herald,** 15 May 1979, sec. B, p. 5.

Goldberger, Paul. "Miami Beach Group Wants To Save Art Deco Hotels". **The New York Times,** 3 February 1979, p. 7.

Hutchinson, Bill. "Miami Beach Renaissance". **Aloft** 11 (November/December 1978): 22-29.

Liss, Robert. "Deco Mania". **The Miami Herald,** 11 February 1979, Tropic Magazine Section, pp. 18-23+.

Olson, Arlene. "Miami Beach: Resort Style Moderne." **The Florida Architect** 27 (January/February 1977): 19-21.

——————. "Streamline: It Isn't Art Deco." **Miami Magazine** 28 (January 1977): 88-91.

——————. "14 Places You Never Noticed In Miami Beach." **Miami Magazine** 31 (January 1978): 50-51.

——————. "Miami Beach Moderne." **The Metropolitan** 1 (August 1978): 22-26.

——————. **A Guide To The Architecture Of Miami Beach.** Miami, Florida: Dade Heritage Trust, 1978.

——————. "Building To Weather The Depression." **Southeastern College Art Conference Review** 9 (Spring 1979): 164-172.

Rimer, Sara. "Victory for Art Deco Proves That the Past Has a Future." **The Miami Herald,** 15 May 1979, sec. B, p. 1+.

Smiley, Nixon. "Game of Golf Changed Miami Beach Skyline." **The Miami Herald,** 16 September 1968, sec. C, p. 1+.

Werne, Jo. "They're Out to Save Old Beach Hotels." **The Miami Herald,** 21 November 1976, sec. K, p. 18-19.

ART DECO and MODERNE

Applegate, Judith. "What Is Art Deco?" **Art News** 69 (December 1970): 39-42+.

Bletter, Rosemarie Haag and Robinson, Cervin. "Skyscraper Style; Art Deco Architecture Re-evaluated." **Progressive Architecture** 56 (February 1975): 68-73.

Bush, Donald J. **The Streamlined Decade.** New York: George Braziller, 1975.

Goldberger, Paul. "Style Moderne-Kitsch or Serious-Is in Vogue." **The New York Times,** 31 January 1974, p. 35+.

Huxtable, Ada Louise. "The Skyscraper Style." **The New York Times Magazine,** 14 April 1974, pp. 58-59+.

Plummer, Kathleen Church. "The Streamlined Moderne." **Art In America** 62 (January/February 1974): 46-53.

Varian, Elayne H. **American Art Deco Architecture.** Catalogue of an Exhibition, November 6, 1974 through January 5, 1975. Finch College Museum of Art, New York.

Williams, Priscilla de F. and Dwyer, Donald Harris. **Art Deco and its Origins.** Catalogue of an Exhibition, September 22- November 3, 1974. Heckscher Museum, Huntington, New York.

ISBN 0 905836 33 2
Library of Congress Catalog Card No. 79 – 55711
© Jewel Stern
   Museum of Modern Art, Oxford 1982.

Catalogue designed by John Coplans
Second Edition printed in Great Britain by the Holywell
Press, Oxford.
Published by the Museum of Modern Art, 30 Pembroke
Street, Oxford OX1 1BP.

A list of all Museum of Modern Art catalogues in print
can be obtained from the Bookshop Manager at the
above address.